Between Chance and Mercy

Poems

JAMES E CHERRY

Between Chance and Mercy

Cover art: "Rhythm Color" by Robert Delaunay
Author photo: James E Cherry

ISBN 978-1-7330898-2-1

Willow Books, a Division of Aquarius Press
www.WillowLit.net

Printed in the United States of America

Contents

Foreword

Enter James E. Cherry's poems to witness a Black male poet's painting of the harshness of nature's and social storms, its cost in loss of landscape or "mangled metal. . ." This humble voice, peers through "75 cent glasses. . ." "in awe. . . holding. . . years."

In one elegy, the poet carries his father's name, "the courage of his calloused hands,. . ." a tribute to his legacy of manhood in crisp images, moving from "union dues. . .assembly lines" from the son who dashed his Dad's hope for the son to college.

One poem, "Freedom," a praise poem/elegy honoring the "61st Regiment of the U.S. Colored Troops, " lays out a litany of images framed by "Freedom" is at once a lyric and a narrative where "Freedom is/ an unmarked grave/ . . . raising a hallelujah." Other elegies of rhetorical questions, readers will never forget: "How does a black mother forgive/ herself for delivering a black baby/ boy to the altar of America?"

The poems of Eric Gardner, Trayvon Marton and George Floyd give concrete cast to hollowed promises of the past, the crushing cruelty of the present for Blacks in America, shots exploding in the back or manhood suffocated.

Another delight and surprise, recreating voices in Black speak, authentically, profoundly of the "folk" from historical record; one narrative in the voice of an enslaved child afraid to be sold, watching Massa get girls "when he think/ aint nobody looking." Another of an old man trying to buy a bottle of hootch. These are priceless testimonies of imagined lives now past, speaking their colored times of "gutbucket blues" that "sanitize troubles." Then, the human condition from Wuhan, China, "our lives languages apart, yet/ the air we breathe. . . ." There's the Black lesson on social distancing "learned . . in holes of ships. . . his white neighbor. . . his name/ across the morning and applaud/that he is alive."

Cherry captures the smallness of life during Corona, the challenge of worship live streamed, then a "Good Friday" elegy at the family gravesite, where he went to "listen. . . allow silence to remind him" who he is.

Cherry's memorable poems enrich us with their brilliance, depth, delight, and haunting truth.

—Dr. Mona Lisa Saloy

Cherry Cherry

—*cento for Mr. James 8/7/2013*

cool days, those we ol' school days

blues trains hug the depot and spades in
red caps salute the new arrivals with a knowing smile

exit onto Ellington & Ella

so hard to sing this new old life

arduous moments of sleep and lethargy
following loss after loss

rainy days drunk with sound
talking to the walls the bed the radio

kickin' those fickle feet into gear and ass follows

roiling rolling onward upward as in Rahsaan
as in the formative pulses of mornings to come
as in the intersection between slick and wicked
as in the space between almost and always

sunny days drunk with sound

certain

*Dear Mr. James, This is the first poem I've written in a year since my world
fell away. The credit is all yours. Thank you.*

Wanda Coleman/Los Angeles

AFTER THE STORM

a red-tailed hawk crowns
a 100 year old oak,
shoulders afternoon light.

From my window, he is witness
to a vortex of wind loosed
upon the earth 24 hours ago.

Across the street, mangled metal
beneath fallen trees was once
someone's sports car dream.

Snatched utility poles dangle
between power lines
and splinters of themselves.

The head of a decapitated
cedar scents my front lawn.
Two of my neighbors were

chased from their homes
by other oak trees
that lost their footing.

Another friend
searches the neighborhood
for his wooden fence.

Calamity has come
to the community, images
on Cable news, other storms

in someone else's grief.
After sunset, the night
will remain unplugged,

            muffled
by its own denseness.

But for now,

the majestic bird watches
me watch him, a feather
                    drifts,

my outstretched hands
a hallelujah to receive it,
before he gathers yesterday

beneath wings, pushes off
into a patch
of blue promise.

ECLIPSE
(08/21/2017)

In minutes, the moon will elbow a cool path
between earth and sun, make a shadow
of afternoon, throw shade
at the knowledge of man, his dominion
over creation.

In a 75 cent pair of glasses, I explore the heavens,
find the sun a ring of fire around itself. I'm listening
for Dizzy's staccato brass to split the sky
or Jesus to step out on a cloud, point
to my name in the book. I would settle
for George Clinton behind the wheel
of the Mothership Connection.

Instead, in four days another year
will pass between this world and me,
55 seasons sifting daybreak from dusk.
Over the decades, my hair has thinned,
my sight bi-focaled and these bones

creak with my rising, sitting. But I remain
in awe of how the planet moves, that I have held
on all these years, have not been thrown
from its surface, waltzing across the universe,
a vertigo of desperation and light.

60th

I woke up on my 60th birthday and knew
I was going to die. Like my father,
two nephews, two brothers in law,

I felt the earth's generational pull
towards the remembrance of dust.
The sum parts of my days

are scattered in the margins of morning
and putting them back together
is not enough.

I stand in judgement of all
that I have written and what the world
has made of it. My words unborn,

progeny to immortalize a life,
cushion the fall of shadows.

THE TOOLBOX

The final hours of the year fall,
robe me in twilight
beneath the hood of an eight-year-old
BMW. My oil-stained fingers slip
between shifting shadows, fumbles
fading afternoon light. I kiss

the skinned knuckles on my left hand,
curse the standard socket in my right,
stomp into the corner of the garage, disrupt
the order of solitude with slamming
drawers, rummaged contents.

Top shelf, right corner: just within reach
on tip toes and the touch of fingertips:
a toolbox. I blow cobwebs
from its metallic heaviness, mites confetti
around my head, rub my hand across its lid
and faded black letters. My father's name.

Three syllables. My fingers recite
the name—my name too--over and over.
I have carried his name across the earth
for six decades. I trace each letter on the box
and from forty-one years of dust rise
the rhythm of his voice and steady footfalls,
the courage of his calloused hands,

his weathered character and dignified deathbed.
I flip the latch, raise the lid.
Turtleneck sweaters, Old Spice, Jack Daniels
and light escapes, reminds me
that I have everything
I will ever need to finish the job.

DREAM OF MY FATHER

My father looks the same as the day he died.
Such is the nature of nocturnal visits. Actually,
he looks like the man who dragged eight hour shifts

of union dues and assembly lines
through the front door at day's end, frowned
at the daily paper, grunted the six o'clock

news, whispered grace over supper
around a square dinner table. I'm at the head
of the table this time. He sits to my left

works a plate of cabbage and potatoes,
wears the same mask the day I quit
the high school basketball team in mid-season,

was caught smoking pot in the basement,
broke the promise of a college diploma
into several pieces. I offer him the roast beef

on my plate, but he says nothing, moves away
from the table and when I rise to run after him,
daybreak catches me around the ankle

leaves me sprawled beside the bed
to count drops of sunlight
spilling from my eyes.

I WANT A UFO

I want a UFO
  to crash land in my backyard
  at 3 o'clock
  in the morning.

I want its occupants to crawl
  from the wreckage, limp
  to my backdoor and rap
  me from sleep.

I want to wave them in (their color
  or gender or the gender they prefer
  will not matter) to cleanse cuts,
  splint sprains, to sit, eat
  leftover collard greens and cornbread.
  Or a bowl of Cheerios.

I want to ask who they are and what
  did they hope to become and what
  color their planet and did it groan
  or rejoice and who in hell
  was flying that flying saucer?

I want to know what on earth
  are they doing in west Tennessee
  on a Saturday night and how do they feel
  about white folks in outer space
  who carry a catechism of colonialism.

I want to know when was the last time
  they bumped into God and was He born
  old and when is his birthday
  and does he ever wear a wrist watch.

I want to ask if they want
  a Dos Equis or a Jack Daniels
  for the road and who's going to pay

me for my roses and azaleas as we stand
under moonlight and magnolias.

I want to know do they believe in humans
    and are they ever disappointed
    and who buries a planet
    when it dies and why are they crying
    as they enter their craft and become
    three lights sucked into the sky.

THE HOUSE ACROSS THE STREET

Sunday morning delivers another Easter
outside my window. I wonder why the Southern Baptists
across the street didn't get the Good News. There is no laughter
of children in pursuit of painted eggs, oversized bunnies bouncing
across manicured lawns, no men milling about in starched collars

after Sunday school or women promenading with price tags
daggling from dresses. The church parking lot is crowded
with open space, a rapture of Buicks and BMW's. Maybe
the aging membership didn't have enough strength
to roll away new stones, only enough patience to wait two days,

or maybe the pastor found an abundance of courage
behind bolted doors of a nearby attic. Or perhaps
there were just too many leaks in that old building.
On this day of new beginnings, I would like to believe
that the entire congregation had an epiphany

minutes before midnight, that church buildings
don't make a church, that each dawn births sufficient grace
to walk through the world, just enough mercy
to return home at the end of the day.

BETWEEN CHANCE AND MERCY

I straighten my necktie
in the rearview mirror, exit
my Ford pickup, enter

Dave's Liquors
where they know my name
and the face of the dead President

I drop onto the counter twice
a week to gather Power
ball tickets, thrust them into my wallet.

It's Sunday and morning
presses upon me with the heaviness
of mortgage payments, doctor bills

and benefits that perish
at the end of the month.
The drive across town pushes me

through the city's gray streets
ends upon a clean swept parking lot.
I enter the Methodist church,

mouth scriptures, revisit old hymns,
kneel at the altar, my outstretched hand,
trembling.

JUNEBUG TOSSES A FOOTBALL IN HEAVEN

The first minute of forever
finds you on a verdant hillside,
cerulean sky around your shoulders

eternal sun rising in your eyes,
Cowboy jersey on your back,
a football gripped across the seams

and sailed across the face of the wind
into your baby brother's hands. We hear
echoes of your voice in thunder

after midnight, new rain on the morning,
the laughter of your children's children.
Our prayers are frequent and numerous,

their answers are slow to return,
only leave the word why
to fill the void. But there is solace

in the truth that you are beyond the pain
that bound you to this place, a cool spot
reserved for you and Bryant to rest

from playing catch
and that daybreak
has never forsaken the horizon.

ALCHEMY

My youngest sister's youngest child
is 35 years old, turns my living room
into a nightclub, my wife and I
its only patrons.

He unpacks his bags from Cincinnati,
wires two turntables and a mixer
into my Samsung soundbar, melds
scratches of Hip Hop with Bebop

polyrhythms until the room sways,
snaps its fingers. He could be mistaken
for a mad alchemist twisting this knob,
sliding that lever. I hear dissonant chords

from Monk's 88 keys, see Ella under a spotlight
at the Apollo, catch armfuls of sheets of sound
from Coltrane's horn. After supper
and between chess moves, we discuss

Octavia Butler, differences between spoken word
and poetry and writing projects of his own.
For a moment, he is 12 years old again and I am
teaching him how to free the rook from itself,

the beauty of a strong queen, that pawns possess
value no matter the game. But now, watching him
anticipate my next move, I learn lessons
of commitment to live one's art and the courage

to do so without the safety net of a 9 to 5. Tomorrow,
at the first sign of daybreak, I will deliver Niles
to a Greyhound station where he will board the morning,
his backpack full of beats and sunrise spread across shoulders.

THRENODY

(after Judy Pennel)
1946 – 2016

The news arrived on a Saturday afternoon
in a place you gave your heart to, a place
that nurtured your soul in return.

The spring day was in full bloom
with all the things you loved: peonies
dogwoods, rhododendrons,

when from the circulation desk, the library
director wanted to know had I heard.
Carrie, just a few days before, informed me

you were packing your possessions
to move from an earthly home
into a heavenly body that would never know

the side effects of chemotherapy or radiation.
But even her warning wasn't enough
to dull the sharp edge of loss or stop shadows

from falling beyond the library's plate glass window.
I sat for an hour or more, wondered
where time had gone with the people

it had taken with it. Everyone has left too soon.
Your laughter cascades from the library's
second floor, sweeps me out of the front door

where I carry the light of your smile
like hope through an overcast day,
shelter against the forsaken night.

MATINS

At daybreak, I gather handfuls of sunlight,
splash them upon face and arms. I robe myself
with the vestments of morning: blue jeans, sneakers

white t-shirt, a ball cap turned backwards my skufia.
My faith has wavered over the years
but has never failed to spark, sputter, catch

the first hours of summer in the roar of small engines.
Within the sanctuary of property lines, my ten year old
mower scents the pines, soothes winter wounds

on roses, lowers the blood pressure of begonias.
Overhead, cardinals knit their voices into the tops of trees
until 100 year old oaks sway and clap hands

in the key of hallelujah. I kneel, remove gloves, pray
for the broken body of an orange and black beetle, meditate
on the distance it has traveled over dry earth, wonder

if it will remember the morning dew.
My neighbor, Charles, emerges on his porch
in work clothes of his own.

I restart my mower, shout
his name above the whir of edged blades.
He squints hard in my direction, holds up his hand.

BOBBY JOE, MONTHS LATER

Three years later, I browse the shelves
of the downtown library in the shadows
of late afternoon where Bobby Joe
materializes among jazz cd's, new book
releases and the New York Times.

He has stumbled through its public doors
dishelved, burdened with bags under arm
as if he were a scale and life had found him
wanting, dreams with holes punched in them.
We slap hands, take the edge off awkwardness

with idle talk, before I tell him that I'd hope
to see him again, that I'd written a book,
Loose Change, that one of the poems was about him.
He shrugs, turns down the corners of his mouth,
rubs his chin, remarks: that poetry is some deep stuff

and that he wanted me to take a look at something.
We seize a corner table near the periodicals where
Bobby Joe pulls a small black and red book
from his bag. I finger the book, peruse a few pages,
flip back to the front cover: Zen Meditation Book.

I tell him that this is in the same family as poetry,
may even be a first cousin, just another way of being
in the world. I give the book back, but Bobby Joe
tells me he has no need for it anymore,
that he could live it, if he wanted to.

I promise to carry a copy of Loose Change
in the trunk of my car for the next time. Bobby Joe
pushes himself up, gathers his bags, nods: Next time
and heads for the new releases, stands
before a wall of books until he becomes one of them.

GRAB 'EM BY THE PUSSY
for Donald J Trump

She's the miracle you held
up to the first light of birth, her name fresh
and wet upon your cheek. She's the joy
jostled upon your knee at a long day's end,

your name an exclamation point in her mouth.
She's the princess you kissed goodnight, tucked
beneath covers after bedtime stories put out the stars.
She's the seventeen year old you waited up for

beyond curfews and corsages of a senior prom,
measured miles one tear at a time to a dorm room
across state lines, composed an epithalamium for the day
you walked her down the aisle where she exchanged

your name for another's. She's a woman now
across town who has delivered a new generation
to your lap with daughters of her own who adore
the stories on granddaddy's tongue after Sunday supper.

She's the flesh of the flesh you swore only death
could separate you from, an extension of the arms
that cradled you in the bosom of sleep, whose breast nurtured
you into who you would become. Your mother's touch

over a hot stove delivered food upon a kitchen table
in the name of the Father, grace and love. These things
you ponder 30,000 feet in the air, stuck in rush hour traffic
or from the back of a bus. You are a man. These are women.

You can do anything.

JOINING THE AARP

You know you're old
the minute you retrieve the package
from your mailbox at the end of the driveway.

Inside, already are cards
with your name in red letters raised
across the front.

You wonder who tipped AARP
to this date where you came screaming
into the ear of the world. Did the cousin you've been

avoiding for the last four months
rat you out in the name of revenge? Or
maybe it was the optometrist's assistant

who sold a copy of your latest prescription
for bifocal lenses. Maybe
your neighbor is an operative who notes

your jog through the neighborhood
has become a leisurely stroll
around the block.

You're convinced your phone has been bugged
for years, that the pharmacist
isn't the only one who knows

about your meds to control
cholesterol and high blood pressure. You
meander back up the driveway

your index finger a letter opener
against the package's edge,
review the application in the mid-morning

sun, realize half a century lies
behind you, that the distance

to your front porch is farther

than it used to be, beyond the door
awaits 10% off hotel visits
and a monthly newsletter.

THE LETTER

The letter from the Attorney General informed me
that last month Orlando Quartez Knox
was a free man. I wonder how many times

has he circled my house in the last thirty days,
the way he did four years ago on a Wednesday afternoon
before crawling through my den window

to ransack the sanctity of peace. That day
the alarm arrested him at the back door; three days later
the police cuffed his freedom.

This day, I weigh the official government letter
against a budding spring day outside
that same den window, wonder if Knox

has read every book in the prison library
to re-invent himself or was made new
falling to his knees, faced pressed

against concrete, submitting his will
to the God of jailhouse confession. Or maybe,
at age 22, he had graduated from the ways

of men much older, had become the criminal
of their harden dreams. I try to forge Knox's face
from memory, but his features refuse to focus.

His height, complexion and hairstyle are lost
to a shifting past where all that remains
of our lives together are three short paragraphs
on State sponsored stationary.

WRITER'S BLOCK
(for Sisyphus)

On Friday, the stone doesn't make it
halfway before it catches me in avalanche
of shadow, leaves me sprawled upon the shores
of the River Styx. I run my fingers through

my hair, gather strength for it
once more to ascend, each muscle taut
with explicit and unsaid tension. Some days,
the sun flashes as I push across my journey,

illuminates image in the clarity of light, pushes me
higher and faster toward the apex. But Zeus
is a motherfucker, causes my foot to slip,
the hillside to crumble. I dust myself off, smile

at the rock that has chosen me to burden.

FREEDOM
(after the 61st Regiment of the US Colored Troops)

Freedom is
    a broken shackle
    rusting between rows
    of Tennessee cotton.

Freedom is
    stealing moonlight
    from swampland, bare footprints
    tracking the north star.

Freedom is
    squalor on the edge of town
    erected from the pen of Abe Lincoln.
    Call me contraband.

Freedom is
    a uniform sewn of Union necessity,
    a blue wool cloak
    for African manhood.

Freedom is
    Six and a half dollars
    less for a colored troop, compound interest
    on insult and disease.

Freedom is
    a regiment of runaways, black faces
    armed with courage and Springfield rifles.
    Johnny Reb enraged in retreat.

Freedom is
    Six hundred hands in surrender
    to Bedford Forrest's bayonets.
    The Mississippi hemorrhages at Henning.

Freedom is
>> an heirloom around Harriet's neck
>> bequeathed to her children's children
>> and those waiting to be born.

Freedom is
>> an unmarked grave
>> on some great gettin' up morning
>> raising a hallelujah

POEM FOR TYRE NICHOLS

I heard a black man cry
for his mother today. Another black man.
Just an ordinary day. Listen.

At the corner of Castlegate & Bear Creek
it's the same slave block howl
after the auctioneer's gavel, southern shrieks

from rope and gasoline, one long moan
exiting Cup Foods, rolling down
Chicago Avenue South.

Its echo will undoubtably follow
and find you next door to yourself
or if you have lost your way

home, will demand to know
how many lynchings does it take
to save my life or that of your own?

How does a black mother forgive
herself for delivering a black baby
boy to the altar of America

except she pluck a handful of sunset
from the Memphis horizon, hold on
until a light gives birth to itself?

*THE NINTH OF AUGUST, 2014
(after Mike Brown who had his hands up and didn't even know it)

It could have been early morning Principe Hill
in Spain, but was afternoon just north of St. Louis,
instead. At your feet lay Shawn Bell, Oscar Grant,
Eric Gardner and to your right the faces
of my nephew, my brother, my son unborn.

The light must have blindfolded your eyes
and you couldn't see any faces, only the barrel
of a .40 caliber gun glinting in Missouri sun.
Their uniforms are always a variation of the same.

And maybe, just maybe, your back against America,
you realized that no amount of bullets could hurt
you anymore, your only regret that no one
stepped forward to offer you a Cigarillo
or was allowed to knell over your body to pray.

*Based on Francisco Goya's painting the Third of May, 1808

I'M SORRY
(Tulsa Oklahoma, April 2 2015)

It's the same familiar words you've heard
after flipping mildewed pages of the Constitution
or 250 years of viewing the world
from the purview of auction blocks. After all,
those words were mid-wife to the songs
you birthed when there would be
no forty acres, mules.

They are familiar as 100 year old sweat
on a sharecropper's brow, the rope burns
around the neck of charred remains when cut
down. After all, these words form scabs,
leave scars after police dogs, water hoses
and billy clubs are long gone.

You have learned to count
these three syllables under leaky roofs
in separate school houses or memorized
their refrain from the back of the bus. After all,
these words erected a ghetto
around your life one brick at a time
until you were fettered by poverty,
helplessness and despair.

They are the same hollow words
that pull the trigger when you are
running away, that shoot you in the back,
will lower you into the earth
and stand over your grave. After all,
they will kick dirt in your face, smile.

I CAN'T BREATHE
(for Eric Gardner)

It has always been difficult
in this place, the air heavy
with the stench from the holes
of ships, suffocating as a plantation
with its rows of cotton 250 years long,
rancid as burnt flesh twisting
from the neck of trees, bitter
as water from white drinking fountains,
the back of the bus or the word "boy," acrid
as fitting the description. Stop. Frisk.

History is a forearm pressed against the throat,
a knee jammed to the back, a head mashed
into the sidewalk and I have learned
from its austere lessons that eternity exists
between inhaling and the act of letting go.

TRAYVON
(02/05/1995 – 02/25/2012)

Storm clouds stalk me
from the corner store.
Its wind snuffs the North Star
just seventy yards from home,
a hoodie protection against falling sky.

I have been detained
on many a night as this, accused
of being someone's suspect, asked
for papers to prove I have not
outrun the scent of hounds.

These are lessons learned
in the pursuit of happiness:
a cell phone, a can of iced-tea,
a bag of Skittles, spilled
shadows against the red earth.

PASS

Most days, you keep your papers in order:
    know to keep both hands on the wheel
    when blue lights strike the rearview,
    know to check your messages in the elevator
    so the white woman next to you can relax
    the grip on her purse, know to avoid restaurants
    whose plush seats feel like Woolworth's lunch counters,
    know the clerks almost by name who trail you
    around department store aisles, know to walk
    across parking lots with keys dangling
    from your hand to disarm more than just car alarms,
    know to smile around the office and measure
    the length of your tongue by the amount of sports,
    cars, weather that rolls off it.

But some days you get caught slipping:
    remember that you are a man, wander too far
    from the plantation with nothing but the blackness
    of your skin reflected in moonlight, suspected
    of searching for the North Star and when asked for I.D.
    you tell them to kiss your Skittles and go fuck themselves
    with a can of iced tea and you are not terribly surprised
    by anything anymore, how a hundred lashes
    across your back feels no different than a single bullet
    exploding inside your chest.

A SURVEY OF AMERICAN HISTORY IN 7 MINUTES & 46 SEC-
ONDS
(after George Floyd)

With guns trained at your temple, they drag you
from your car (make/model will not save you)
handcuff the remaining minutes of your life, slam you
face first into the street. Any street or nigger will do.
They kneel for as long as it takes for blood & urine
to fill a gutter or God and your mother to answer a prayer.
They do not cut off your genitals to formaldehyde
in some museum's collection. Instead, they stand
around and make you watch your own death,
make others unsee a history that daily reinvents itself,
teaches you that you are responsible
for your own noose and gasoline, blames you
for not knowing the difference
between fire and air.

HIGHER GROUND
(for Therese Patricia Okoumou,
who scaled the Statue of Liberty, July 4th, 2018)

Against the Manhattan skyline, a dark hand rises.
Late afternoon catches its ascent between sun
and shadow. This dark hand

scales a cloudless sky one blue rung at a time,
has cornered freedom between New York Harbor
and the fourth of July. This dark hand

has seized Liberty by the heel, will not
toss her head first into the Hudson or slash her
chiseled features. This dark hand

is not gloved in suicide sequins, only a determined grip
to whisper in her windswept ear that somewhere
upon the doorstep of America there are those yearning

to breathe free behind detention wire, tempest-tossed
mothers whose breasts ache for newborn lips, mounds
of mylar weeping beyond the golden door of a cage.

A dark hand rises, refuses
to surrender until history crumbles
into a lie or stone eyes give birth to tears.

HOUSE OF GOD

There is a for sale sign on the House of God
where I denied Jesus three times in the Easter play, later
proclaimed Him the Christ rising from a watery grave
on a baptismal morning, after that, wondered where was the Savior
when the pastor ushered both parents into the earth, then waited
at the altar to lift a veil and become the flesh of another.

There is a condemned sign on the House of God
where its hard to tell pimps from preachers
who covet Coupe de Villes, currency and concubines,
hard to tell the difference between proselytes and prostitutes
who choke on the wafer, gulp unfermented Koolaid.

There is a vacancy sign on the House of God
in a black neighborhood in the black section of town
where other black churches clutter every other corner
of every other street, where syringes and bullet casings
spring from the soil, where the naked, hungry and weary
make pillows out of church house steps.

There is a for sale sign on the House of God
where behind locked doors and state of the art security
the Messiah hangs from a mural with open arms
that measure the distance between grace and mercy,
just wide enough to bring four walls down upon itself,
for buzzards to regurgitate the rubble.

THE SEGREGATED WORD

My sister calls from Nashville, asks where is she
in my latest collection of poems, *Loose Change*,
her voice cloudy as a winter afternoon

in 1968 where we climb steps
to the public library, enter into its sacred space,
follow the memory of our feet

to the "Colored" section. I pet Clifford
the Big Red Dog, look for my mom
from the top of Jack's Beanstalk, pat my tummy

for a house of chocolate cake
instead of a gingerbread one. I watch my sister
and others, their Black faces bowing

at the altar of study, fidget away
from them into a land peopled by more books
where a white lady with a sharp nose

and round glasses rules over them.
"Get back over there. Nigger."
Her words welt across my face,

take aim at the other cheek before my hand
is in Marcia's and we're back
behind the safety of color lines.

She rearranges me in my seat, strides
across the aisle where her words grab handfuls
of the white woman's hair, their voices

crescendo of curse and epithet. She reappears
with a smile and an armful of books, instructs me
to "read these" as I open bound leather,

where a solitary tear staggers from my eye
onto the red nose of a reindeer, its glow
neon against the night, my hands grasping

for stars and the moon around Rudolph's neck,
my life, strapped upon the back of the wind.

A BLACK BOY WAS HERE
(Gil Scott-Heron Historical Marker Dedication)

Just south of Jackson, a black boy learns love
in his grandmother's arms, her hands a comfort
and refuge through segregated streets.

On Cumberland Street, a black boy grows
precocious at his grandmother's table
from bread, Blackness and words

of a poet who has known rivers, sits him
upon a rickety stool in front of a hand
me down piano for lessons on 88

broken keys until the room blossoms
into handclaps and hallelujahs. A black boy
in his bed past midnight, music from Beale

scratches against his window invites him
outside to walk among the stars. A black boy
enters an all white house of learning

on a cold January morning to teach a nation
what it should have known long before 1954.
A black boy discovers his grandmother

has taken up wings, left her body
in the only home he'd ever known. One day
he too would leave this place for good

and carry this small southern town all over the world.
Today, Jackson, Tennessee genuflects, honors
the years that forged a black boy into a black man

his image now adorns this city's walls,
his spirit rests upon this city's shoulders.

09/23/2022

NOCTURNAL POETICS

Amiri Baraka burst all the windows out of my dream.
I sat in a circle of poets where he towered
in the midst of us; Randall Horton was there.

Baraka advised that we read, practice, make certain
our words lindy-hop across the page. He admonished
against over revision, to not limit our minds

to what we think and to never imitate anyone,
not even ourselves. He reminded us
to consider the world, construct form

to compliment content and that poetry is
the bastard of politics. Baraka touched
my shoulder, encouraged me to seek

that smile at the bottom of the world
and with a wink of the eye boarded daybreak
as if it were the A-Train headed uptown, going home.

THE PRODIGAL
(for Amiri Baraka)

The blood was still fresh in the Audubon ballroom
when you shed the skin of Greenwich Village,
slipped into the comfort of African Dashikis.

You left behind a world of Beats and Bohemia,
went searching for your life with nothing
but the poems on your back and found it

on the doorstep of 125th Street. Blues people
pulled your coat on corners of consciousness. You
crafted masterpieces of their anger, doubts, dreams,

hung them on the wall of a movement. Later,
you moved beyond 1965, but Harlem
was forever over your shoulder, that same Harlem

that stood on the edge of a brilliant morning
recognized you from afar, embraced your return
with the open arms of a fiery dawn.

MISSISSIPPI: A HISTORY

The road from Jackson winds south, cuts
through cotton fields of west Tennessee
over hills rolling with soybeans
across the Mississippi state line.

Its two lanes push through low hanging clouds
on a January afternoon towards Oxford. I want
to shake hands with William Faulkner, take
a photograph with Eudora Welty, sip

corn liquor at the feet of Robert Johnson, sit
on the Square on a Saturday afternoon.
But, just past Rust College, the body
of Emmit Till floats past my windshield,

Goodman, Schwerner and Chaney rise
in my rearview mirror, the engine
of a passing pickup explodes like the report
from de la Beckwith's rifle. On campus,

the smell of gunpowder from Kennedy's troops
and Confederate reinforcements still singe
the air. Governor Barnett walks the grounds
with papers in his hand. James Meredith

has been chiseled out of 1962. The gray
of afternoon drifts to dusk and somewhere
the roar of a crowd hoists Archie Manning
upon its shoulders. The road from Oxford

plows north, a two hour drive before me
the Mississippi night behind me and a history
that catches me somewhere in between,
awaits all the places I'll ever know.

MIGRATION SERIES
(for Jacob Lawrence, Panel 1)

It could have been Goree
with clearly marked points
of destination, a mass of huddled Blackness
in tatters of winter apparel
dragging suitcases of Southern possessions,
the sum of American dreams, a movement
through century old portals
into the crowded silence of whiteness
falling off the edge of the world, faint sounds
of hope echoing near the bottom.

ELIZA WOODS
(08/18/1886)

Most nights, you can find Eliza Woods downtown,
sitting on the base of our monument to the Confederate Dead,
digging into the dirt under the moonlight, excavating
for a relic of justice. Speak her name,
she'll raise her head, scan the horizon that swallows
your voice with echoes of curses, rebel yells,

shotgun blasts that leave exit wounds in the sky.
Sheriff Person could not protect you, Eliza.
White men with torches, blood lust in their eyes
ripped the clothes off your back and drove you
from a jail cell into the August night. The carnival

had come to town: White kids cartwheeled the stars,
white women jostled babies on hips and reminisced
about the last time, their men slobbered a flask between them
and music square danced from HC Bryant's Hardware.
Did you recognize the faces, Eliza--black faces
made to assemble and bow to a history of degradation and fear,

lessons taught from a crumbled Constitution in the hands of Jim Crow?
Forced to confess poisoning Mrs. Jesse, you spoke silence,
would not be the last to be slapped, spat upon, driven
from one judgment place to another. Your sex would not save you.
The color of blackness, unforgiveable. Your flesh

bruised along cobblestones, scrapped raw on Jackson streets,
strangled in a noose and nailed to a tree where gunshots
targeted your body. The mob roared. The night sighed.
In the morning, makeshift grave clothes entombed you.
Shafts of sunlight filtered your remains, cast shadows
on a silver crucifix, trampled in the broken earth.

A SLAVE CHILD'S CONFESSION

Mammy, is Ole' Massa gwin'er sell us tomorrow?
Yes, my chile.
Whar he gwin'er sell us?
Way down South in Georgia.

I wasn't the only child
on Massa Doak's fifty acres. There was Dicy,
Esther, Nelly, Phillis and Andy.
My name Henry.

We was south east of Alexandria
long before the whole land was named
after a president a long ways from here.
By time I turned eight, I did the same thing

the grown folk did: chopping cotton, slopping hogs,
tending to what Massa's wife, Mrs. Patsey, needed
tending to. I was always hungry. I felt
like a pig at a trough. I learned to scratch

and curse the other kids over potatoes, grits, pot likker.
Our black bellies all shiny and swollen. My ribs
shined through the holes in my shirt. The only thing
the younger kids wore was they naked bodies.

In the shadow of day, we climbed trees, galloped
stick horse or Hide the Switch, where we hide
a hickory and whoever finds it would chase
the other kids to try to whip them. We slept

in one room, side by side with another family.
A fireplace in between. Pa made us
a table, benches and a bed. Before Sunday go
to Meeting, we go down to the river. It tell us

what we look like. Some nights, Massa come
get Esther or Phillis when he think
aint nobody looking. Or maybe he don't care.
The grown folk say the world is big and round.

But far as I can tell it ends at the edge of a cotton field.
It has to be flat 'cause everybody thats ever been
sold I aint never see again. The grown folk say
change is coming, that the town wont be called

Alexandria no more. Will be named after a general.
I say that's ok. Nobody ever ask me what I want
to be when I grow up. I say that's ok too.
My name is written in the book.

When Massa die, I belong to his son, Alanson Fielding.
Me and a dark gray horse.

*Steven Mintz, "Childhood and Transatlantic Slavery," in Children
and Youth in History*

SHANNON STREET SPEAKS

I went down on Shannon Street
Now to buy some alcohol
I told him to put it half-full a-water
But they didn't put it in any drop at all.

Sonny Boy Williamson, 1938
 Jackson, Tennessee

First of all, I wasn't no cousin to Beale
or Bourbon's nephew and was never
in the family of brights lights, jooks
or all-night parties. That's just wishful talk
been handed down from tongue to tongue.

This is what you need to know: I was born
between 1872 & 1875 to Thomas Shannon,
a saloon keep and first sheriff of this county.
I grew from dirt road to brick, was known
more for livery stables than live music,

where blacksmiths outnumbered blues musicians.
I was a colored street in a colored neighborhood
in a segregated town and some of my residents
did about as well as colored folk could do:
Andrew Cain & Thomas Davis turned an old

cotton warehouse into a saloon around the corner.
Not far from there, Isaac H Anderson built
from the ground up an ice cream pallor, office
space, pool hall and barber shop all under
the same roof. The Black Mason would hang

out there for a while. The Colored Methodists
Publishing House was a neighbor and they still
in the history books today. But if you ever had trouble
finding me, there were landmarks to get you there:
Haynes Fish Market, Armour Meat Company,

Marvin Jones Seed Store. The north side of me
was pretty much business and commerce, the south end
folks just trying to survive. And if you cant find
the Farmer's Market today, you cant find nothing.
And then there was that lil harp blowing Negro

who couldn't hold his liquor and made me famous
in a song. Tried to tell him 'bout that drinking
and I'm sorry things ended the way they did. I love Sonny Boy
Williamson. Always will. Its true. You could plug the hole
in your soul with gutbucket blues, sanitize your troubles

with a pint of Hootch. If you could find it.
But I wasn't about to tell you where. Matter of fact,
I've probably ruined your notion
of what I used to be. Its hard to tell what's real
and what's not anymore. You don't even have to believe

me. I'm just an old man with potholes for knees
and vacant lots where my hair used to be.
But I'm still here. There ain't nobody else I'd rather be.

PRELUDE TO AN ETHNIC CLEANSING
Treaty of Old Town, October 19, 1818

Twenty-four months later, the white man is back.
He is always back, this same white man. Sharp Knife.*
We bled shoulder to shoulder in his battles

against the British. He supplied bullets
for our guns turned on those who looked
like us. This time he comes with another

piece of paper, the same piece of paper
we sign over and over. It honors nothing—
past nor future, just broken promises.

Time forgets and refuses to mend. Some say,
our leaders, Itawamba Mingo and his brother
Tootesmastube, pocketed a bag of silver

before handshakes. It really does not matter.
Sharp Knife's words echo down generations:
"The hunt is over, the game is gone."

Either our brains or our signature
was going on that piece of paper. We surrendered
the earth roamed by the spirit our ancestors,

a culture inscribed on our tongues,
our souls for money in the storehouse of our tears.
Aba Binni'li'* could not save us

from a bruised sky, bare feet and blankets,
a winter's journey across a history
that always ends where it begins.

*Sharp Knife. Andrew Jackson
*Aba Binni'li'. Chickasaw name for God

THE NEWS FROM WUHAN

The professor from Central China
Normal University informs me about life
in Wuhan, that for the past two months
it consists of walls built by hands of quarantine,

dreams that dance beyond bedroom windows.
Luo Lianggong has known heartbreak,
lost much when the Sichuan earth moved
in 2008 and chooses to document suffering

and how it shapes the human condition.
Today, his email wishes my family health
and peace and asks for a poem, maybe two. I think
about Lianggong long after I respond yes

and hit send, our lives languages apart, yet
the air we breathe a wafer upon our tongues
and to trouble a few lines of verse
is another way of saying I love you.

03/15/2020

SOCIAL DISTANCING

Africans in America have always known
the meaning of social distancing long before
the lungs of the world struggled for air.

They learned definition in holes of ships,
at the end of master's lash, at the feet of Jim Crow,
in neighborhoods redlined with poverty,

at houses of worship (that's what Malcolm said),
by a Governor's decree, under a judge's gavel,
the end of a rope. Now, days are measured

by six feet of separation, regardless of skin or gender
red state or blue state, this virus
come to do what amendments to a Constitution

could only dream of---remind us of a common future.
Hours are spatial and disorienting: Filet mignon
from Chandelier is delivered in paper bags, curbside.

The marque at the Empire Theatre blindfolded. Planet
Fitness' parking lot distended and slovenly. The clippers
at Pearl's Barber Shop refuse to sing. This Sunday

my neighbor, Shane, a white man, stands
on his front porch and stretches in the cool, crisp air.
I raise my window, shout his name

across the morning and applaud
that he is alive.

03/22/2020

LOVE IN THE TIME OF CORONAVIRUS

The infrared thermometer files the temperature
of my thoughts. I log in and answer no
to sore throat, dry cough, shortness of breath.
I'm given hand sanitizer to cleanse my alienation.
The world is smaller than it has ever been,

feels so much wider than it need be. Lately,
I've been wondering how friends & fellow poets
are faring through days of isolation and I email
Frank in Kentucky, HC in KC, Jeanie in Alabama,
Kimberly in Australia, Patty just across town.

I drink wine into the late hours, my dreams
edgy and febrile with right hands of fellowship,
a reassuring pat on the back, the passion of a hug.
My awakening burns for a kiss on the cheek
rendered from mercy or devised in the name of deceit.

03/27/2020

PALM SUNDAY

                                        Nothing
stirs the city: no wayward horns
of essential autos, the color and crescendo
of children's laughter, a donkey's hoof
scraping asphalt and dust. The Governor's *shelter*

at home arrests cries of Hosanna, Hosanna.
No one searches scripture at my Baptist Church
or lifts hallelujah from the choir's loft
or baptizes in the Name. Instead

the homily is live-streamed, an app
for your tithes and offerings.
I wonder after all these years if Jesus would die
for my sins just one more time, wonder

how many palm leaves it takes to cover
the distance between me and God,
if my worship this Sunday morning
will become curses by Friday afternoon.

04/05/2020

GOOD FRIDAY

Late afternoon divides Parkway Memorial
Cemetery between sun and shadow, my family
and the bones of others. A south wind gathers April

at my feet, plants Spring in my eye. I stand
over gravesites, my nephew on the left, my mother
on the right and my father between. My hands bear

no flowers nor my tongue weighed with words. Instead
I have come to listen to the dash that separates dates
they were born from transitions to dust.

This burial ground sways, stumbles toward the horizon.
I lean upon the earth, strain to hear an echo of my name,
allow silence to remind me who I am.

EASTER

The wind reaps rain and thunder,
sows them upon rooftops of sleep, troubles
the foundation of morning. An unbroken
grayness seeps beneath windowsills, spreads
Easter across my bedroom floor.

In this the year of our Lord, all resurrections
have been quarantined. His blood and body
available for curbside pickup. Six feet separates
shame from salvation.

I stare at the ceiling until it blows away
and the house explodes. I salvage grace
from the rubble, pray that lightning
consumes all that remains.

04/12/2020

THE LONG HAULER

One year after, 700,000 are lost,
faces from the evening news, others
who have left indelible traces upon this life.

Each morning, I guesstimate antibodies,
take 1000 mg of Vitamin C to compensate
the missing. A sore arm and acute sadness

my only side-effect from a vial of panacea.
My alienation wears an N95 against the vicissitudes
of variants before I step foot upon daybreak.

At the workplace, I take the temperature
of isolation once a day and it returns twice
as high as the day before. I have learned

to camouflage loneliness with a walk
in the park, a restaurant patio, friends
six feet apart. By five o'clock

it is midnight already. I unlock
the front door, close the world behind.
After supper and the sorting of mail

the numbing of alcohol, sounds
the house makes when nudged
by evening hours, an echo somewhere

between solitude and desperation.

THE MASK

I sleep with a mask each night, wake
in the morning to poet the city's
pandemic streets. Paul Laurence Dunbar,

you know who I am: The same
cheek turned at a five & dime lunch counter,
eyes bloodied on a Sunday bridge

against the Alabama sky. But this mask,
a century later, is what remains
of an assassinated dream, the smoldering ashes

in an ex-hustler's speech, a president's
post-racial society. This mask explodes,
shotgunned after a neighborhood jog,

glocked in a bedroom after midnight
from eight no-knock bullets. This mask seeds
stereotype in Dollar Store clerks upon entrance, blooms

fear of a natural born suspect in baby blue eyes.
I exit with disinfectant spray, readjust the mask,
my only protection against a fetid nation

in search of a remedy for its past,
a vaccine against its whiteness.

A REPLY TO BROTHER JAMES E CHERRY

There is no chance

Life will have mercy on us

We are born here
Were borne here
Our Blackness both a stain
And a shining on these killing fields
Called America

We must all face the martial music
Of Whites falsely proclaiming that
Their alabaster proclamations
Offer some kind of earthly salvation

Have mercy

No matter. We will lift every voice
We will sing. We will dance.
No matter what is done to us
We will be better than any trouble
Yesterday or tomorrow visits upon us.

There is no chance, only
The love and struggle we wage
To make this world better
And more beautiful than when
We arrived, birthed
In the various colors and shades
Of our Blackness

—Kalamu ya Salaam

About the Poet

James E Cherry is the author of two novels, three volumes of poetry and a collection of short fiction. His latest novel, *Edge of the Wind,* was a *Foreword Review* 2016 Book of the Year Finalist for Fiction. Cherry has an MFA in creative writing from the University of Texas at El Paso and has been nominated for an NAACP Image Award, a Lillian Smith Book Award and a Next Generation Indie Book Award. He is an Adjunct Professor of English at the University of Memphis-Lambuth and resides in Tennessee with his wife, Tammy. Visit him at www.jamesEcherry.com.

Milton Keynes UK
Ingram Content Group UK Ltd.
UKHW010851280324
440101UK00001B/167